The Story of a Special Day
Volume 13

January 13

January 13 is the thirteenth day of the year. There are 352 days remaining (353 in leap years) until the end of the year.

by Michael Dobson

Timespinner
Press

This book is also available in e-book form for Kindle, e-pub devices, and other formats from your favorite online booksellers.

For more information about the series, about us, or about your special day, please email us at editor@timespinnerpress.com.

Look for other volumes in *The Story of a Special Day,* coming often. See www.timespinnerpress.com for details and for the most recent information.

Table of Contents

For the definition of "O.S.," "N.S.," "CE," and "BCE" used with some dates , see the section "On Names and Dates."

Quote of the Day

"I have but one passion: to enlighten those
who have been kept in the dark, in the name
of humanity which has suffered so much and
is entitled to happiness. My fiery protest is
simply the cry of my very soul."

Émile Zola, novelist and journalist
His famous letter on the Dreyfus Affair (*J'accuse!*) was
published in *L'Aurore* on January 13, 1898

Today
in
History
THE.17.
ACL.
MAGNA
January 13

Portrait of Henry Howard, Earl of Surrey, by Hans Holbein the Younger (Courtesy Royal Collection)

What Happened on January 13?

From the creation of great works of engineering and art, to devastating wars and natural disasters, thousands of years of history have left their mark on each and every day of the year. Here are some important events that occurred on January 13. (Illustrated items are shaded.)

1547 — Henry Howard, Earl of Surrey, is known as one of the **"fathers of the English sonnet."** Cousin to **Anne Boleyn** and Catherine Howard, both queens to **Henry VIII**, he was sentenced to death January 13, 1547, accused of **trying to usurp the throne**.

"The Last Stand of the 44th Regiment at Gundamuck, 1842," by William Barnes Wollen (Massacre of Elphinstone's Army)

1842 — A British force of more than 16,000 is repeatedly attacked as it attempts to withdraw from Kabul, Afghanistan. In what becomes known as the **Massacre of Elphinstone's Army**, only one European and a few sepoys reached safety.

1898 — Dreyfus Affair: Accusing the French government of anti-Semitism and the illegal jailing of Alfred Dreyfus, writer **Émile Zola** publishes a dramatic letter, **"J'Accuse,"** in the French newspaper *L'Aurora.*

"J'Accuse," by Emile Zola, appeared January 13, 1898

1910 — The **first public radio broadcast** takes place when engineer and inventor Lee de Forest transmits a program a live opera performance featuring Enrico Caruso to a small number of radio receivers stationed at different locations in New York City.

Cover Story
Introduction of the Frisbee (1957)

On January 13, 1957*, the original Frisbee Flying Disc by Wham-O (then known as the "Pluto Platter") went into production.

The origin of the modern flying disc dates back to the late 1930s when inventor Fred Morrison and his girlfriend (later wife) Lucille started tossing a popcorn can lid back and forth on a beach near Los Angeles. The popcorn can lid didn't last very long, so the couple began experimenting with other shapes, settling on cake pans.

Fred Morrison demonstrates the "Pluto Platter"

---

* Some sources say January 23, but whether that's the day the first ones are shipped or the day they go into production is unclear.

One day, a beachgoer offered the couple 25¢ for their cake pan. "That got the wheels turning," Fred Morrison said in a newspaper interview, "because you could buy a cake pan for five cents, and if people on the beach were willing to pay a quarter for it, well — there was a business."

Their business, Flyin' Cake Pans, lasted until World War II, when Morrison joined the Army Air Force, becoming a P-47 fighter pilot. He was shot down and spent 48 days as a prisoner of war.

During that time, he also learned something about aerodynamics, and after a few disappointing early trials, eventually designed and patented the Pluto Platter. He sold the rights to the Wham-O toy company.

When Wham-O learned that college students in the northeast US started a craze by tossing pie pans made by the Frisbie Pie Company, Wham-O grabbed the name. A new marketing executive, "Steady Ed" Headrick, redesigned and rebranded the Pluto Platter as a "professional model" Frisbee, and created the idea of Frisbee sports.

Frisbie pie tin (Photo: Doug Coldwell, CC BY-SA 3.0)

While flying discs are generally called "frisbees," the name remains a trademark of Wham-O. Frisbees remain popular today, and Wham-O's product is in the National Toy Hall of Fame.

An Australian Shepherd catches a Frisbee at the Toledo Metro Parks Dog Festival, 2008 (Photo: Sally Wehner, CC BY-SA 2.0)

1968 — Following his 1955 hit "Folsom Prison Blues," performer **Johnny Cash** performs two live shows at **Folsom State Prison** in California, the basis for his hit album *Folsom Prison Blues*.

Cover of the Johnny Cash album *Folsom Prison Blues*.

1982 — Shortly after its takeoff from Washington's National Airport, **Air Florida Flight 90** crashes into the 14th Street Bridge and falls into the Potomac River, killing 78.

1990 — Upon assuming the office of Governor of Virginia, Douglas Wilder becomes the **first African-American governor** of any state since Reconstruction.

"January," by Simon Bening, from *Labors of the Months*

Quote of the Day

"Don't judge a man by the tales of others."

G. I. Gurdjieff, mystic and spiritualist
born January 13, 1872?

Births
and
Deaths
THERI
ACA
MAGNA
January 13

Robert Stack in The Untouchables (1960). Robert Stack was born January 13, 1919

Notable January 13 People

With the current world population at about seven billion people, on average about 19 million people also celebrate their birthdays on January 13 — and that isn't counting millions and millions who came before! No matter when you were born, you share your birthday with many special people whose accomplishments (and occasionally embarrassments) have been noted as part of history.

In this section, you'll meet fascinating people who share your birthday. They're organized by what they're famous for, and then in reverse chronological order from most recent to earliest. Those who are shown in photographs or artwork have a box around them. We don't have photos of everyone, so please forgive us if your favorite person is missing.

Some of these people you've heard of, others will be new to you, but they all make up an important part of the reason that January 13 is a truly special day!

Statue of Paddington Bear at Paddington Station, London (Photo: "Shrinkin' Violet," CC BY-SA 2.0). Paddington Bear creator **Michael Bond** was born January 13, 1926

Who Was Born on January 13?

Business and Industry

Alfred Fuller, founded the Fuller Brush Company, noted for its door-to-door salesforce , which inspired the 1948 film *The Fuller Brush Man. (1885)*

Government and Law

Salmon P. Chase, American politician and judge who served as Governor of Ohio and Secretary of the Treasury before becoming the 6th Chief Justice of the US Supreme Court. He was the face on the no-longer-used US $10,000 bill. *(1808)*

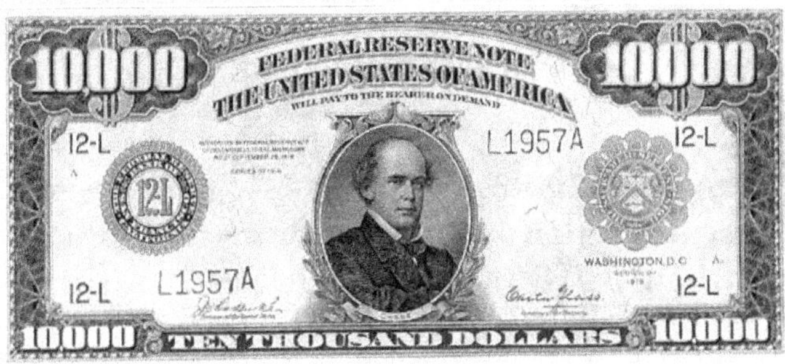

The US $10,000 bill featuring Salmon P. Chase

Journalism and Letters

Nate Silver, statistician and writer who analyzes elections and baseball, and produces the FiveThirtyEight blog. Successfully called the outcomes of 49 of the 50 states in the US presidential election of 2008; named one of the "World's 100 Most Influential People" by *Time* magazine. *(1978)*

Jay McInerney, American novelist known for his 1984 best-seller *Bright Lights, Big City. (1955)*

Michael Bond, British author best known for creating the *Paddington Bear* franchise. (1926) *(Photo page 12.)*

Ted Willis, British playwright and screenwriter listed in the Guinness Book of Records as the most prolific writer for television, also wrote 34 plays and 39 feature films. Awarded a life peerage (Baron Willis) by the British government. *(1914)*

Zhou Youguang (周有光), Chinese economist and publisher known as "the father of Pinyin" for leading the development of a standard system for pronouncing Chinese characters in western languages, now considered the standard method of doing so. *(1906)*

Clark Ashton Smith, known for his fantasy, horror, and science fiction stories, and for his friendship with fellow writer H. P. Lovecraft. *(1893)*

Horatio Alger, Jr., American writer best known for his "rags to riches" novels for young adults, in which poor young men rise from their humble backgrounds to become successful and secure. *(1832)*

Music

Trace Adkins, country singer whose number one hits include "Ladies Love Country Boys" and "You're Gonna Miss This." *(1962)*

Trevor Rabin, singer-songwriter best known as a guitarist in the band Yes, for which he wrote "Owner of a Lonely Heart." *(1954)*

Sophie Tucker, popular early 20th century singer, actress, and radio personality known as "The Last of the Red Hot Mamas" and "The First Lady of Show Business." *(1887)*

Sheet music for "Ev'rybody Shimmies Now," featuring **Sophie Tucker** and Her Five Kings of Syncopation (1918)

Performing Arts

Ruth Wilson, actress known for the 2006 film *Jane Eyre,* the 2012 *Anna Karenina,* and 2013's *Saving Mr. Banks. (1982)*

Orlando Bloom, actor known as Legolas in the *Lord of the Rings* films and Will Turner in the *Pirates of the Caribbean* franchise. *(1977)*

Nicole Eggert, actress on such sitcoms as *Charles in Charge* and *Boy Meets World. (1972)*

Shonda Rhimes, television producer and writer who created such shows as *Grey's Anatomy, Scandal,* and *How to Get Away With Murder. (1970)*

Patrick Dempsey, actor best known as "McDreamy" Shepherd in the TV series *Grey's Anatomy. (1966)*

Penelope Ann Miller, actress who appeared in such films as *Biloxi Blues, Big Top Pee-Wee,* and *Kindergarten Cop.* (1964)

Julia Louis-Dreyfus, actress and comedienne best known for her work on *Saturday Night Live* and *Seinfeld. (1961)*

Brandon Tartikoff, NBC network president who developed such hit series as *Hill Street Blues, Law & Order, Family Ties, Cheers, Seinfeld,* and many others. *(1949)*

Richard Moll, played the bailiff on the sitcom *Night Court. (1943)*

Gwen Verdon

Charles Nelson Reilly, comic actor and television personality who appeared on *The Ghost & Mrs. Muir* and numerous game shows. *(1931)*

Ian Hendry, British actor best known as the first partner of John Steed in the television series *The Avengers. (1931)*

Gwen Verdon, actress and dancer who won four Tony award for Broadway roles, also known for her collaborations with her husband, director-choreographer Bob Fosse. *(1925) (Photo page 17.)*

Rosemary Murphy, received an Emmy for her role in *Eleanor and Franklin,* appeared in numerous films including *To Kill a Mockingbird. (1925)*

Robert Stack, actor best known for his Emmy-winning starring role in the television series *The Untouchables;* appeared in the film *Airplane!* and hosted *Unsolved Mysteries. (1919) (Photo page 10.)*

Kay Francis, stage and film actress who was the number one female star and the highest-paid female actress during the 1930s. *(1887)*

Philosophy and Religion

George Gurdjieff, mystic who promoted the idea of achieving a higher state of consciousness to achieve full human potential. Influenced people as disparate as Timothy Leary, P. L. Travers (*Mary Poppins*), and Frank Lloyd Wright. *(1866?[†]) (Photo page 20.)*

[†] Various sources give the year as 1866, 1872, or 1877.

Kay Francis and Mitzi Mayfair on a 1943 USO tour (Photo: Ann Rosener)

Science and Medicine

Eric Betzig, American physicist who shared the 2014 Nobel Prize in Chemistry for work in super-resolved fluouescence microscopy. *(1960)*

Rakesh Sharma, Indian Air Force pilot who flew on the Soyuz T-11 mission, becoming the first Indian in space. *(1949)*

Sydney Brenner, South African biologist who shared the 2002 Nobel Prize in Physiology or Medicine for his contributions to understanding the genetic code. *(1927)*

Wilhelm Wien, German scientist who received the 1911 Nobel Prize in Physics for his work in heat radiation. *(1864)*

George Gurdjieff

Sports

Max Whitlock, British gymnast who earned five Olympic medals at the 2016 Rio de Janeiro games. *(1993)*

Vitaly Scherbo (Віталь Шчэрба), gymnast who won six Olympic Gold Medals and the only male gymnast to have ever won a world title in all eight gymnastics categories. *(1972)*

Mark O'Meara, golfer who won numerous tournaments on the PGA Tour; elected to the World Golf Hall of Fame *(1957)*

Art Ross, influential hockey player and executive from the early years of the 20th century until the 1950s; member of the Hockey Hall of Fame. *(1885)*

Art Ross (Courtesy Hockey Hall of Fame)

The "Dodge City Peace Commission," 1883. From left to right: (standing) W. H. Harris, Luke Short, Bat Masterson (seated) Charlie Bassett, **Wyatt Earp,** Frank McLain, and Neil Brown.

Who Died on January 13?

Art and Photography

Lord Snowden, noted British photographer and filmmaker, married to Princess Margaret, sister of the Queen. *(2017)*

Jan Brueghel the Elder, innovative Flemish painter, son of Pieter Brueghel the Elder. *(1625)*

"A Summer Landscape with Harvesters," Jan Brueghel the Elder (1610), courtesy Toledo Museum of Art

Crime and Punishment

Wyatt Earp, gambler and lawman who served as deputy town marshal in Tombstone, Arizona, where he took part in the gunfight at the O.K. Corral. *(1929)*

Government and Military

Hubert Humphrey, US senator from Minnesota and Vice President of the United States during the administration of Lyndon B. Johnson. *(1978)*

Hubert Humphrey

Schuyler Colfax, Indiana journalist and businessman who served as Speaker of the House of Representatives and Vice President of the United States. *(1885)*

Wilhelm Mauser, German weapon designer and manufacturer who developed and produced the Mauser rifle. *(1882)*

Gaius Marius, military leader who held the office of Consul seven times, an unprecedented achievement. Made major military reforms of the Roman legions; uncle of Gaius Julius Caesar. *(86 BCE)*

"Gaius Marius on the Ruins of Carthage," John Vanderlyn (1842)

Journalism and Literature

James Joyce, Irish novelist and leading figure of the modernist avant-garde in literature, wrote several important works including *A Portrait of the Artist as a Young Man, Ulysses,* and *Finnegans Wake. (1941)*

James Joyce, by Djuna Barnes

Edmund Spenser, English poet best known as the author of the epic *The Faerie Queen. (1599)*

Music

Teddy Pendergrass, singer-songwriter who came to fame as lead singer of Harold Melvin & the Blue Notes before embarking on a solo career.

Andre Kostelanetz, conductor of the New York Philharmonic and other orchestras, pioneered what became known as "easy listening" music. *(1980)*

Donny Hathaway, blues and soul singer-songwriter who wrote "The Ghetto, "Where is the Love," and "For All We Know." *(1979)*

Stephen Foster *(right)*, American songwriter known as "the father of American music;" composed such standards as "Oh! Susanna," "Camptown Races," "My Old Kentucky Home," and "Beautiful Dreamer." *(1864)*

Performing Arts

Dick Gautier, played Hymie the Robot in *Get Smart* and Robin Hood in the TV comedy *When Things Were Rotten. (2017)*

Patrick McGoohan, actor best known for his spy roles in the 1960s television series *Danger Man* (*Secret Agent* in the US) and the surreal classic *The Prisoner. (2009)*

Patrick McGoohan

Frank Shuster, Canadian comedian best known as part of the comedy duo Wayne and Shuster. *(2002)*

Marcel Camus, French film director best known for his award-winning 1959 film *Black Orpheus (Orfeu Negro). (1982)*

Ernie Kovacs, highly influential American comedian, actor, and writer whose *Ernie Kovacs Show* pioneered a visually experimental comedy style that has been widely copied. *(1962)*

Ernie Kovacs (right) with wife and co-star Edie Adams from the television show *Take a Good Look*

Religion and Philosophy

George Fox, founded the Religious Society of Friends, commonly known as Quakers. *(1691)*

Science and Technology

Paul Villard, French chemist and physicist who discovered gamma rays. *(1934)*

Alexander Popov (Алекса́ндр Попо́в), Russian physicist considered to be the inventor of radio[‡] in several eastern European countries; Radio Day in the Russian Federation is celebrated each May 7 to commemorate one of his technical achievements. *(1906[§])* *(Photo next page)*

Sports

Johnny Podres, named MVP of the 1955 World Series for pitching a shutout in Game 7 against the Yankees to help the Brooklyn Dodgers win their only World Series before moving to Los Angeles. *(2008)*

[‡] Elsewhere, Guglielmo Marconi is more often given that recognition.

[§] Popov was born January 13, 1906, according to the modern "New Style" Gregorian calendar. However, because Russia converted from the "Old Style" Julian calendar later than the rest of Europe, his date of birth is also listed as "O.S. December 31, 1905," the same date on the earlier calendar. For an explanation of the Julian and Gregorian calendars, see "What Day of the Week is January 13?"

Joe McCarthy, manager who led the New York Yankees to seven World Series championships in the period 1931 to 1946; member of the Baseball Hall of Fame. *(1978)*

Alexander Popov

Quote of the Day

"Television is a medium, so called because it is neither rare nor well-done."

Ernie Kovacs, comedian
died January 13, 1962

Holidays
Around
the World
CHEM
ACC
MAGNA
January 13

Miss Rose Cade, "Queen of the Lemons," was nominated to be southern California's "Swat the Jinx" girl in 1920

January 13 Holidays and Celebrations

If you're looking for a reason to take your special day off, you should know that every single day is a holiday somewhere in the world! Here's some of what you can celebrate on January 13!

Friday the Thirteenth

While January 13 doesn't come on Friday every year, sooner or later, every 13th day of the month eventually lands on the dreaded last day of the week.

Friday the 13th is considered an unlucky day in many (but not all) Western nations. Both the number 13 and Friday have a history of being thought unlucky, so when you put the two togethe.... The idea that Friday is unlucky seems to be a maritime superstition — sailors believed it was unlucky to start a voyage on a Friday.

As far as the number 13 goes, there are a number of theories.One theory is that it refers to the 13 people around the table at the Last Supper, one of whom (Judas) would shortly betray Jesus. Others point out that on Friday, October 13, 1307, the Knights Templar were arrested, and many of them were later tortured and killed. In Norse mythology, Loki becomes the 13th guest when he crashes a party in Valhalla; the fallout results in the death of Baldur.

Fear of the number thirteen is common enough that a psychological condition, *triskaidekaphobia,* is named for it! (Fear of Friday the 13th is *paraskevidekatriaphobia.*)

(Photo: W. J. Pilsak, CC BY-SA 3.0)

According to some researchers, between 17 and 21 million people in the US alone are bothered by Friday 13th. Fear of thirteen is so common that many tall buildings skip 13 when numbering floors — over 80 percent of high-rise buildings in the US alone! Many hotels, hospitals, and airports don't have rooms or gates numbered 13 either.

Perhaps some of the bad luck associated with Friday 13th is self-inflicted. Fewer people drive on Friday 13th, but there are more accidents.

In Spanish-speaking countries, as well as in Greece, they worry about Tuesday 13th (*martes trece*) instead —though either way, January 13 qualifies. In Italy, though, 13 is a lucky number — but watch out for Friday the 17th!

In most of Asia, the number four is considered unlucky — the Chinese words for "four" and "death" are similar. Buildings in Asia may have a 13th floor, but often don't have a 4th floor.

General Events

Constitution Day (Mongolia)

The nation of Mongolia honors its constitution on January 13.

Democracy Day (Cape Verde)

The Cape Verde islands celebrate Democracy Day on January 13.

Korean-American Day (US)

The United States commemorates the contributions of Korean-Americans on January 13.

Liberation Day (Togo)

The nation of Togo celebrates Liberation Day, marking the military coup that brought Étienne Eyadéma to power in that country, which took place January 13, 1967.

Stephen Foster Memorial Day (US)

An official US federal observance commemorates the date Stephen Foster died, and has been observed since 1967.

Sidereal Winter Solstice's Eve celebrations (various South Asian and Southeast Asian cultures)

Ending the six-month Dakshinayana period on the traditional Hindu calendar, traditional celebrations are held in several nations: Boghi, Lohri, and Uruka, among others. Because the calendar matches are not exact, in some years these are celebrated January 14.

Food Holidays

In the United States, almost every day of the year is dedicated to a particular food. Sponsored by manufacturers, retailers, farmers, or simply fans, these days are often proclaimed by the President, Congress, state governors, or mayors. Given that there are more different foods than days of the year, some days honor more than one kind of food!

In the US, January 13 is **National Peach Melba Day** *(photo)*. It's a dish of peaches served with vanilla ice cream, raspberries, and sauce. Interestingly, peach melba is related to Melba toast, because both are linked to a famous 19th century opera singer, Nellie Melba. She was very slender in her youth, so the dessert was created. Later in life she gained weight, so the same chef created Melba toast for her!

In addition, the entire month of January is used to celebrate numerous foods.

- California Dried Plum Digestive Health Month
- Fat Free Living Month
- National Hot Tea Month
- National Oatmeal Month
- National Slow Cooking Month
- National Soup Month
- National Baking Month
- National Fat Free Living Month

And while we're on the subject of food, January is also **Weight Loss Awareness Month**, in case you've already forgotten those New Year's resolutions.

Nellie Melba, by Rupert Bunny

Religious Feast Days and Holidays

Malanka (Маланья), (Russia, Ukraine, Belarus)

Known as "Generous Eve," this folk holiday is celebrated on January 13, the traditional date for New Year's Eve on the Julian calendar** The eve is celebrated with carolers going door to door.

Saint Days

Each day in the year is a feast day for various saints. They are somewhat different in western Christianity (Catholicism and many forms of Protestantism) and in eastern (Orthodox) Christianity.

In *Western Christianity*, January 13 is the feast day of Saints Veronica of Milan, Elian, Hilary of Poitiers, and Mungo.

In *Eastern Orthodox Christianity*, it is also the commemoration of Saints Potitus, Andrew of Trier, Agricius of Trier, Viventius, Erbin of Dumnonia, Remigius of Rheims, Kentigern, Enogatus, Gumesindus, Servusdei, Berno of Cluny, and Irenarchus the Recluse. (These people are honored on December 31 by "Old Calendrists."[††])

[**] For an explanation of different calendar types, see "What Day of the Week is January 13?"

[††] "Old Calendrists" use the Julian, rather than the Gregorian, calendar for liturgical purposes. For an explanation of different calendar types, see "What Day of the Week is January 13?"

Honorary Months

Presidents, Congresses, and nations around the world issue proclamations recognizing particular months to honor certain causes. These events generally fall in January, though honorary months do come and go. Holidays established by states and nonprofit organizations are listed if verified. If not otherwise specified, all months are US. There is some variation from year to year; some celebratory months get added and others get dropped. Two places to get up to date information are the current edition of *Chase's Calendar of Events* or the website Brownielocks. Here are some honorary designations for January.

- Adopt a Rescued Bird Month
- Bath Safety Month
- Be Kind to Food Servers Month
- Birth Defects Month
- California Dried Plum Digestive Month
- Cervical Health Awareness Month
- Financial Wellness Month
- Get Organized Month
- International Child-Centered Divorce Awareness Month
- International Creativity Month

- National Braille Literacy Month

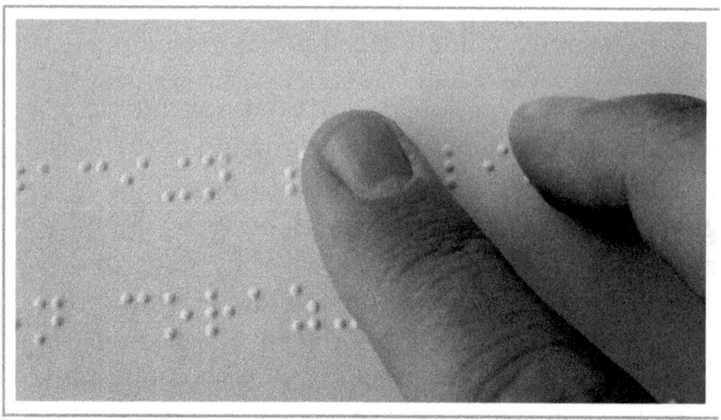

A person reading a braille book, for **National Braille Literacy Month** (Photo: Antonio X Alonso CC BY-SA 2.0)

- National Clean Up Your Computer Month
- National Codependency Awareness Month
- National Mentoring Month
- National Polka Music Month
- National Poverty in America Awareness Month
- National Skating Month
- National Thank You Month
- National Volunteer Blood Donor Month
- Slavery and Human Trafficking Prevention Month
- Stalking Awareness Month
- Teen Driving Awareness Month
- Train Your Dog Month (also Walk Your Dog Month)

Moveable and Multi-Day Events

Some events take place over a specific week or time period. Start and finish dates may vary from year to year. Some events occur on different days each year (such as "fourth Saturday of a month"). These events sometimes take place on or include January 13.

- Lee-Jackson Day (Friday before the third Monday)
- Children's Day (Thailand) (second Saturday)
- National Sanctity of Human Life Day (third Sunday)
- Sinulog (Philippines) (third Sunday)
- World Religion Day (third Sunday)

Week Long Celebrations that Sometimes Include January 13

- Cuckoo Dancing Week
- National Soccer Coaches of America Week
- Hunt for Happiness Week

Just For Fun

Anyone can make up a holiday, and many people do! These holidays are unofficial, and some of them come and go, but here are a few more reasons to celebrate on January 13!

- Blame Someone Else Day
- Make Your Dream Come True Day
- Public Radio Broadcasting Day

Quote of the Day

"It's easy to kill a movie. Just move it to January."

Mike Myers, as "Dr. Evil"
from the *Austin Powers* movies

45

"January," from the *Brevarium Grimani* by Simon Bening (c.1510)

January: The First Month

That blasts of January
Would blow you through and through.
　　　　　　　— *William Shakespeare*, The Winter's Tale

January wasn't always the first month in the year. In ancient Rome, March was the first month until about 450 BCE. Even after January became the official first month in the calendar, Romans still counted dates from the inauguration of the consuls, March 15 and May 1.

In the Middle Ages, Christian feast days were used to start the new year, including March 25 and December 25. It wasn't until the 16th century that European nations made January 1 the official start of the new year. (This was called "Circumcision Style" because January 1 was also celebrated as the Feast of the Circumcision of Jesus.)

The name January (*Ianuarius*) is derived from the Roman god Janus, the god of beginning and transitions. Janus gives his name to the Latin word for door (*ianua*), because January is the door to the year. Janus is normally portrayed as having two faces, one looking toward the future and one toward the past. In spite of that, the goddess Juno was the patron of that month.

In both the Julian and Gregorian calendars[‡‡], January is the first month of the year and one of seven months with 31 days. In the Northern Hemisphere, January is the coldest month of the year, and in the Southern Hemisphere, it's the warmest, equivalent to the Northern Hemisphere's July.

January in Other Cultures

The month of January has different names in different languages. Some nations use calendars other than the Gregorian, and their months may overlap with January. In lunar-based calendars, such as the Islamic calendar, months move through the seasons. Still, many languages often have a word for January itself.

Albanian: Janar

Anglo-Saxon: Wulf-monath

Arabic (Egypt, Sudan, Yemen): يونأغيناير (*yanāyir*)

Arabic (Levant): حزيركانون الثاني (*kānūn al-thānī*)

Arabic (Libya): الصهنار (*aynu n-nār*)

Arabic (Algeria and Tunisia): جأينجانفي (*Jānfī*)

Arabic (Morocco): غيناير (*yanāyər*)

Azerbaijani: Yanvar

Basque: Urtarril

Bulgarian: януари (*januari*)

[‡‡] To learn more about the different calendar types, see "What Day of the Week is January 7?"

Chinese: 一月 (Cantonese: *yātyuht*; Mandarin: *yīyuè*; Taiwanese: *it-goeh*)

Corsican: Ghjennaghju

Croatian: Siječanj

Czech: Leden

Finnish: Tammikuu (oak moon)

French: Janvier

German/Danish/Norwegian/Slovenian: Januar

Greek: Ιανουάριος (*Ianouários*)

Haitian Creole: Janvye

Hebrew: ינואר (*yanû'ar*)

Hindi: जनवरी (*janvarī*)

Hungarian: Január

Irish (Gaelic): Eanáir mí Eanáir

Italian: Gennaio

Japanese: 一月 (*ichigatsu*), 睦月 (*mutsuki*)

Kazakh: Қаңтар (*Ķaņtar*)

Korean: 일월 (*ilweol*)

Lithuanian: Sausis

Maori: Kohitātea

Old English: Se æfterra Gēola

Polish: Styczeń

Portuguese: Janeiro

Russian: январь (*janvar'*)

Scottish Gaelic: am Faoilleach

Sesotho: Pherekgong

Slovene: Prosinec

Spanish: Enero

Swahili/Dutch/Swedish: Januari
Swazi: Bhimbidvwane
Thai: มกราคม (*makarakhom*)
Turkish: Ocak
Vietnamese: 腩乂 (*tháng một*)
Walloon: Djanvî
Welsh: Ionawr
Yiddish: אויגוייאַננואַר (*yanuar*)
Zulu: uJanuwari

Mengapa?   Zašto?
为什么呢？
Por quê? Чаму?
Чому?
كيون؟
Poukisa?   Per què?
Miks?
Tại sao?   Bakit? Kial? למה?
Waarom?   Hvers vegna?
どうして？ ?סאוורא
Niyə?
Warum? Dlaczego? Pourquoi?
Ինչու?   Зашто? چرا؟ Quid?
Cén fáth?   Pam?
ຍ່ບໍ່ມ?
Zergatik?   Miért?
Kwa nini?   Proč?
Hoekom?
De ce?   Kodėl?   क्यों?
เพราะเหตุใด   Защо? Why?
Perché?   Miksi?
لماذا؟   Prečo?   Varför?
Γιατί;
Għaliex?
¿Por qué? Pse?
왜? Почему?
Зошто?
Kāpēc?   Neden?
Hvorfor?   為什麼呢？

January Sayings and Superstitions

Here are some sayings and superstitions associated with the month of January.

New Year Superstitions

- It's important to kiss those dearest to us at the stroke of the New Year to keep their affections for the next twelve months.

- The new year must not be seen with bare cupboards. Stock up on supplies and make sure there's plenty of money in ever wallet in the home.

- Do not begin the new year with the household in debt.

- The first person to enter your home after the stroke of midnight will tell you the kind of year you will have.

- Do not let anything leave your house on the first day of the year, not even garbage.

- Start your year off with good luck by eating hoppin' john, a dish made with black-eyed peas and rice (southern United States).

- Wear something new on January 1.

- Be sure to open the door at midnight to let the old year escape.

- Babies born on New Year's Day will always have good luck.

January Wedding Superstitions

- A January bride will be a prudent housekeeper, and very good tempered.

- Married in January's hoar and rime/Widowed you'll be before your prime.

- Married when the year is new, he'll be loving, kind and true.

January Symbols

Birthstone: Garnet, representing constancy.

Soviet postage stamp showing a geologist finding garnets

Birth Flower (Britain): Carnation, representing love, fascination, and distinction

Vase with Red and White Carnation on a Yellow Background,
by Vincent van Gogh

Birth Flower (America): Carnation or Snowdrop (*Galanthus*)

A New Year's greeting card with snowdrops

Birth Flower (China): Plum blossom (*prunus mume*)

Red Plum Blossom (Photo: Frank Gualtieri)

Birth Flower (Japan): Camellia

Camellias (Clara Maria Pope)

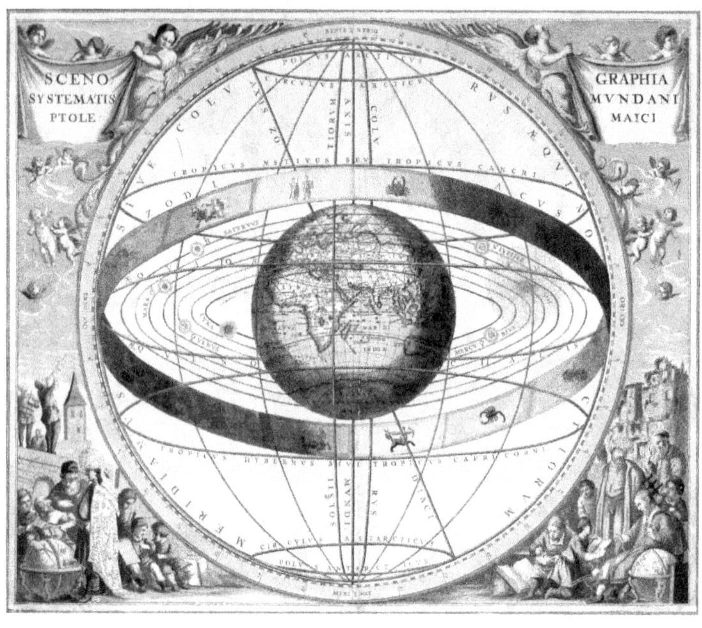

Scenography of the Ptolemaic Cosmography, by Johannes van Loon, based on Andreas Cellarius's *Harmonia Macrocosmica*, 1660

January 13 Zodiac Signs

From the perspective of someone on Earth, the Sun appears to move through the sky throughout the year, along a path astronomers call the *ecliptic plane*. The ecliptic plane is divided into twelve constellations, known as the zodiac, based on traditionally observed patterns of stars. On your birthday, you can't see your constellation, because it's in the daytime sky.

The zodiac was first developed by Babylonian astronomers about 2,500 years ago. Because they were unaware that the Earth wobbles like a spinning top (known as *precession*), they didn't make allowance for the fact that the Sun's path through the zodiac changes over time.

That means there are now two sets of dates for your birth sign. The *tropical dates* are the original Babylonian dates; the *sidereal dates* tell you where the Sun actually appears as it moves along its annual path.

For January 13, the tropical sign is **Capricorn** and the sidereal sign is **Sagittarius.**

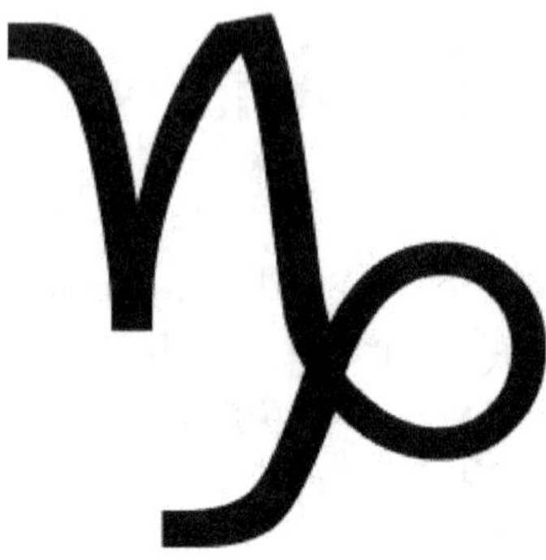

Capricorn

Tropical December 22 to January 20
Sidereal January 15 to February 14

The origins of the constellation Capricorn date back to Sumeria and Babylonia. Based on Enki, the Sumerian god of wisdom and waters, Capricorn has the head and upper body of a mountain goat and the lower body and tail of a fish. The mountain goat represents ambition and intelligence, the fish represents passion and spirituality.

An earth sign, Capricorn is ruled by the planet Saturn. They are often thought to be responsible, patient, ambitious and loyal, but can sometimes be seen as conceited, distrusting, and unimaginative. Capricornians are supposed to be compatible with Taurus, Pisces, and Virgo, but not with Aries, Sagittarius, or Leo.

Sagittarius

Tropical November 23 to December 21
Sidereal December 16 to January 14

The centaur (half-man, half-horse) Chiron was famous as a healer and as an archer. He tutored Achilles, Jason (of Argonaut fame), and Hercules. Unfortunately for Chiron, Hercules accidentally shot him with an arrow that had been dipped in hydra poison. He was unable to find a cure, so gave up his immortality to free Prometheus, and died. In recognition of his sacrifice, Zeus placed him among the stars.

In astrology, Sagittarians are known for their independence and craving for adventure and excitement. They are encouraging and kind, but sometimes lack commitment. They are supposed to be compatible with Aries, Leo, and Libra, but not with Taurus, Scorpio, or Capricorn.

Illustration by Edward Penfield

What Day of the Week is January 13?

On what day of the week does January 13 fall?

Surprisingly, this isn't an easy question. Because the calendar year is 365 days long (366 in leap years), it doesn't divide evenly by the seven days of the week.

Also, the Earth goes around the Sun in about 365-1/4 days, so a calendar tends to drift over time. That's why the same date falls on different weekdays in different years.

This is made even more complicated by a change in calendars that took place in 1582. Our modern calendar has its roots in ancient Rome, in a calendar reform conducted by Julius Caesar. Caesar commissioned mathematicians to attack the problem, and they came up with the idea of leap years, and thus standardized the calendar for centuries to come. This was called the Julian calendar.

Over time, however, the small errors in Caesar's calculation compounded. That's why Pope Gregory XIII commissioned the Gregorian calendar, used in most of the world today. Some countries converted in 1582, when the calendar was first developed; some converted later; other still haven't changed.

Gregorian and Julian aren't the only types of calendars. The Hebrew year, the Islamic year, and many other calendars are used in different parts of the world and among different people.

You can convert Gregorian dates to other calendars, including the Hebrew calendar, the Islamic calendar, and even the Mayan calendar by visiting the Fourmilab Calendar Converter at http://www.fourmilab.ch/documents/calendar/.

Chinese calendar systems are quite complex and have changed several times; a full discussion is far beyond the scope of this book. If you're interested, you can find information here: http://www.hermetic.ch/cal_stud/chinese_cal.htm.

On Names and Dates

Historians use "CE" (Common Era) and "BCE" (Before the Common Era) instead of the more common "AD" (Anno Domini, or Year of Our Lord) and "BC" (Before Christ), reflecting the fact that the year-numbering system established by the Gregorian calendar is used throughout the world in many countries not culturally Christian.

The CE/BCE designation dates back to at least 1708, and has been adopted as a standard by the United Nations and the Universal Postal Union. Because this series of books covers events and people of all nations and cultures, we use the CE/BCE terms.

The abbreviation "O.S." ("Old Style") on some dates refers to the fact that the Russian Empire did not switch from the Julian "Old Style" calendar to the Gregorian "New Style" calendar at the same time as the rest of Europe, and therefore some figures and events have two dates.

Also, in the Julian calendar in England in the 16th century, the year began on March 25 rather than January 1. To avoid confusion with Gregorian dates, dates between January and March were often written using both years.

People and events whose original names are not in the Western alphabet have their native names (where possible) in the appropriate script shown in parenthesis. If you are using an e-reader to access an electronic version of this book, all characters don't always display on all devices.

A 50-year brass perpetual calendar.

Quote of the Day

"Time is an illusion, lunchtime doubly so."

Douglas Adams,
from *The Hitchhiker's Guide to the Galaxy*

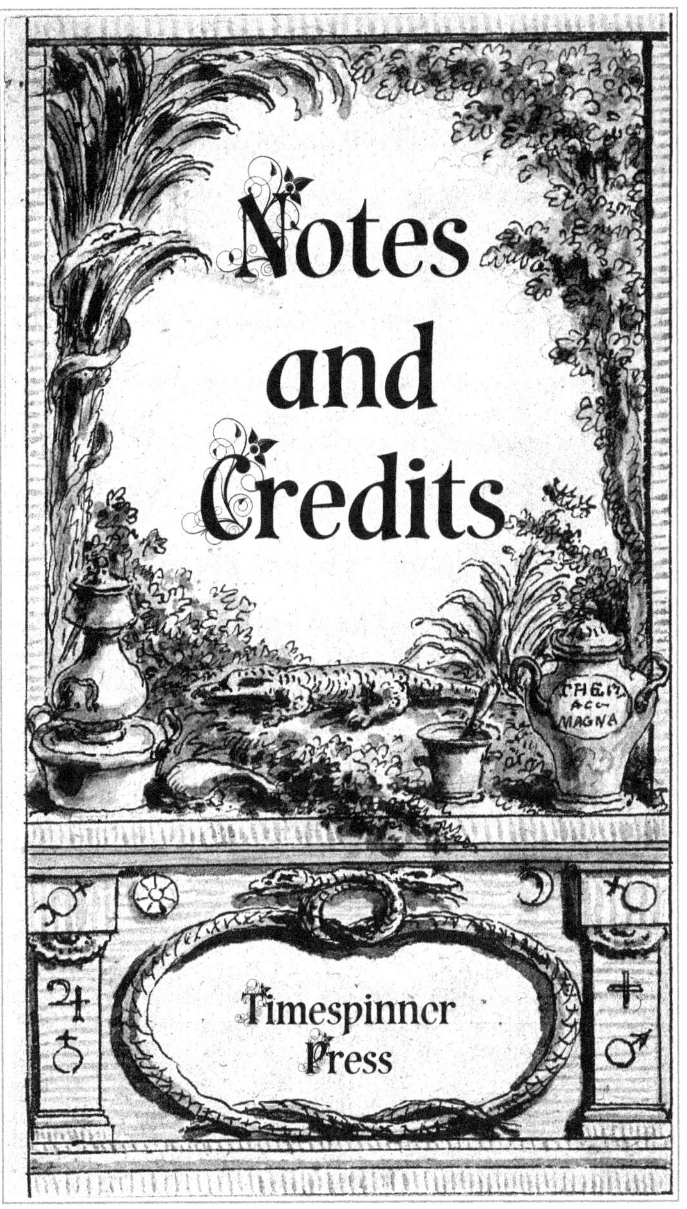

Notes
and
Credits

Timespinner
Press

Cartoon by John T. McCutcheon

Copyright, Credit, and Contact

Follow Us

Our blog "This Day in History" (http://timespinnerpress.com/this-day-in-history/) features short articles on events and people associated with each day, and updates several times each week. Also subscribe to the "Quote of the Day" at http://timespinnerpress.com/quote-of-the-day/. You can get daily links by following us on Facebook at TimespinnerPress, or on Twitter as @sidewisethinker.

Contact Us

Find an error or a format problem? Want information about the series, about us, or about when the volume for your special day might be available? Please email us at editor@timespinnerpress.com. (We also take requests if your special day isn't yet complete. Please give us at least six weeks' notice if possible.)

Sources

We owe a great debt to Wikipedia, which is our first stop for research. We attempt to make independent confirmation of all important dates and facts through a variety of other sources.

Other sources we frequently use include the Library of Congress; "on this day" listings from *Encyclopedia Britannica*, the *New York Times*, and the BBC; Omniglot for the names of months in other languages; *Chase's Calendar of Events*; and, of course, the always essential Google.

All art and photographs are either in the public domain, used under a Creative Commons license, or with a "fair use" justification, and most frequently come from Wikimedia Commons and the Library of Congress Prints and Photographs Division.

Attribution is provided where possible, or as requested by the copyright owner, or when there is particular historical significance, listed below. For information about any particular illustration or photograph, please contact us.

Credits

1. The 2014 photograph "Fairy Playing" was taken by Vladimir Pustovit. It is used here under CC BY-SA 2.0.

2. The illustration of the month of January used on the back cover is from the French Gothic illuminated manuscript *Les Très Riches Heures du duc de Berry* by the Limbourg Brothers, Jean Colombe, and an intermediate painter whose name is lost to history.

3. The box graphic used on the first page is from a 1916 pamphlet entitled "Divorce versus Democracy" authored by G. K. Chesterton, originally published in London by the Society of St. Peter and St. Paul. It is in the public domain in the US because it was published prior to 1923, and is in the public domain in all countries (including the country of origin) in which the copyright time is the author's life plus 70 years or less.

4. The graphic design for the section pages in this book is from a design originally created for a pharmacy label. It is from Wellcome Images (ICV No 11073, photo V0010813), and is used here under CC BY-SA 4.0.

5. The 1533 "Portrait of Henry Howard, Earl of Surrey" by Hans Holbein the Younger is in the public domain because its copyright has expired. It is part of the Royal Art Collection.

6. The 1898 painting "The Last Stand of the 44th Regiment at Gundamuck, 1842," by William Barnes Wollen is in the public domain because its copyright has expired.

7.   The front page of the January 13, 1898, issue of *L'Aurora* is in the public domain because its copyright has expired.

8.   The late 1950s publicity photograph of Walter Frederick (Fred) Morrison demonstrating the "Pluto Platter" is in the public domain because it was first published in the US between 1923 and 1977 without a copyright notice. Traditionally, publicity photographs are not copyrighted because of the way in which they are intended to be used.

9.   The 1995 photograph of a Frisbie pie tin was taken by Doug Coldwell, and is used here under CC BY-SA 3.0.

10. The 2008 photograph of a dog catching a Frisbee was taken by Sally Wehner, and is used here under CC BY-SA 2.0.

11. The cover of the Johnny Cash album *Folsom Prison Blues* is most likely copyrighted by its creator or publisher, and is used here under "fair use" provisions of the copyright code. It illustrates a significant historical event, no free media alternative exists, the image is of a size and resolution unsuitable for the creation of counterfeit goods, and its use here does not impair the owner's ability to profit from the product.

12. The painting "January" by Simon Bening, from his *Labors of the Months,* was created in the first half of the 16th century, and is in the public domain because its copyright has expired.

13. The 1960 publicity photograph of Robert Stack from *The Untouchables* is in the public domain because it was first published in the US between 1923 and 1977 without a copyright notice. Traditionally, publicity photographs are not copyrighted because of the way in which they are intended to be used.

14. The 2015 photograph of the statue of Paddington Bear at London's Paddington Station is by "Shrinkin' Violet," and is used here under CC BY-SA 2.0.

15. The US $10,000 bill is ineligible for copyright and is therefore in the public domain. Fraudulent use of images of US currency is a violation of counterfeiting laws. It is legal to publish images of US currency as long as the image is smaller in size than the actual bill and that the illustration is one-sided.

16. The sheet music for "Ev'rybody Shimmies Now" was published by Charles K. Harris in 1918. It is in the public domain because its copyright has expired.

17. The 1954 publicity photograph of Gwen Verdon is in the public domain because it was first published in the US between 1923 and 1977 without a copyright notice. Traditionally, publicity photographs are not copyrighted because of the way in which they are intended to be used.

18. The 1943 photograph of Kay Francis and Mitzi Mayfair on a USO tour was taken by Ann Rosener. It is in the public domain as a work created by an employee of the US government as part of that person's official duties. It is in the Library of Congress, digital ID fsa.8b06470.

19. The photograph of George Gurdjieff is in the public domain as a work created by an employee of the US government as part of that person's official duties.

20. The photograph of Art Ross was taken between 1907 and 1918, and is in the public domain because its copyright has expired in both the US and Canada.

21. The 1610 landscape by Jan Brueghel the Elder is in the public domain because its copyright has expired. The original can be found in the Toledo Museum of Art.

22. The 1883 photograph of the Dodge City Peace Commission was taken by Camillus S. Fly. It is in the public domain because its copyright has expired.

23. The official portrait photograph of Vice President Hubert Humphrey is in the public domain as a work created by an employee of the US government as part of that person's official duties.

24. The 1842 print "Gaius Marius on the Ruins of Carthage" by John Vanderlyn is in the public domain because its copyright has expired. It is from the Library of Congress collections, digital ID pga.00037.

25. The portrait of James Joyce was created by Djuna Barnes and was originally published in the April 1922 issue of *Vanity Fair*. It is in the public domain in the US because its copyright has expired.

26. The 1860 photograph of Stephen Foster is in the public domain because its copyright has expired.

27. The screenshot from the theatrical trailer for the 1962 film *All Night Long* is in the public domain because it was first published in the US between 1923 and 1977 without a copyright notice.

28. The promotional photo for the television show *Take a Good Look* is in the public domain because it was first published in the US between 1923 and 1977 without a copyright notice. Traditionally, publicity photographs are not copyrighted because of the way in which they are intended to be used.

29. The portrait photograph of Alexander Popov was taken prior to 1885. It is in the public domain both in its home country of Russia and in the US because its copyright has expired.

30. The 1920 photograph of Miss Rose Cade is from the Keystone View Company. It is in the public domain because its copyright has expired.

31. The photograph of a calendar showing Friday the 13th was taken by W. J. Pilsak, and is used here under CC BY-SA 3.0)

32. The 1902 painting of Madame Melba by Rupert Bunny is in the public domain because its copyright has expired. The original is in the National Gallery of Victoria, Melbourne, Australia.

33. The photograph of a person reading a braille book was taken by Antonio X. Alonso in 2009. It is used here under CC BY-SA 2.0.

34. The 1815 woodcut of a Regency era wedding proposal is in the public domain because its copyright has expired.

35. The painting *January* is from the *Brevarium Gremani*, circa 1510, and is in the public domain because its copyright has expired.

36. The graphic of "Why" in several languages was created in 2011 by "Maierstrahl," and is used here under CC BY-SA 3.0.

37. The 1968 USSR postage stamp "Prospecting Geologist with Found Diamond and Red Crystals-Pyropes (Garnets)" is not an object of copyright according to Part IV of Civil Code No. 230-FZ of the Russian Federation (2006).

38. The 1886 painting "Vase with Red and White Carnations on a Yellow Background" by Vincent Van Gogh is in the public domain because its copyright has expired.

39. The German New Year's greeting card was made circa 1900.
    It is in the public domain because its copyright has expired.

40. The 2006 photograph of a red plum blossom (*prunus mume*)
    was taken by Frank Gualtieri, who released the photograph
    into the public domain.

41. The illustration of camellias by Clara Maria Pope is from
    Samuel Curtis' *Monograph on the Genus Camellia*, published
    in 1819. It is in the public domain because its copyright has
    expired.

42. The celestial sphere is from *Scenography of the Ptolemaic
    Cosmography*, by Johannes van Loon, based on Andreas
    Cellarius's *Harmonia Macrocosmica*, 1660. It is in the public
    domain because its copyright has expired.

43. The 1906 automobile calendar is by Edward Penfield, and is
    in the collection of the Library of Congress Prints and
    Photographs Division. It is in the public domain because its
    copyright has expired.

44. The 50-year perpetual calendar photograph is in the public
    domain.

45. The cartoon by John T. McCutcheon is from his 1905
    collection *The Mysterious Stranger and Other Cartoons by John
    T. McCutcheon*. It is in the public domain because its
    copyright has expired.

46. The 1896 postcard "January" by Eugène Grasset is in the
    public domain because its copyright has expired.

License Description and Terms

Aside from material purely in the public domain, photographs and other material in this book are used under specific licenses permitting free use, usually with an attribution requirement. For full text and terms of these licenses, click or enter the appropriate links below. If you believe there is an error in the copyright status or attribution of any of these images, please email us.

- Creative Commons Attribution 2.0 Generic (CC-BY 2.0): http://creativecommons.org/licenses/by/2.0/deed.en
- Creative Commons Attribution-Share Alike 3.0 Generic (CC-BY-SA 3.0): http://creativecommons.org/licenses/by-sa/3.0/
- Creative Commons Attribution-Share Alike 2.5 Generic (CC-BY-SA 2.5): http://creativecommons.org/licenses/by-sa/2.5/deed.en
- Creative Commons Attribution-Share Alike 2.0 Generic (CC-BY-SA 2.0): http://creativecommons.org/licenses/by/2.0/deed.en
- Creative Commons Attribution-Share Alike 1.0 Generic (CC-BY-SA 1.0): http://creativecommons.org/licenses/by-sa/1.0/deed.en
- CC0 1.0 Universal (CC0 1.0) Public Domain Dedication (CC0 1.0) http://creativecommons.org/publicdomain/zero/1.0/deed.en
- GNU Free Documentation License (GFDL): http://en.wikipedia.org/wiki/Wikipedia:Text_of_the_GNU_Free_Documentation_License
- License Art Libre (Free Art License): http://artlibre.org

January, by Eugène Grasset

Other Books from Timespinner Press

The Story of a Special Day

Michael Dobson

A series of (eventually) 366 volumes covering everything that happened on your special day! Events, births, deaths, quotes, holidays, and much more. It's like a birthday card they'll never throw away!

US$7.95 print / US$2.99 ebook.

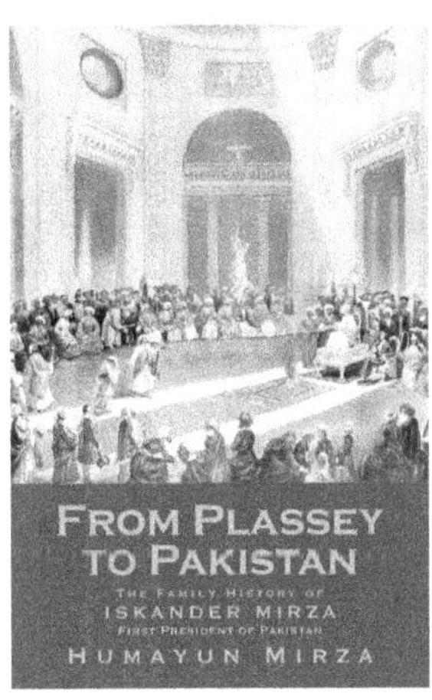

From Plassey to Pakistan

Humayun Mirza

The history of British Colonial India and the formation of Pakistan from the unique perspective of the son of Pakistan's first president and last of the royal line of Bengal, Bihar, and Orissa! This unique historical document tells the inside story of this distinguished family, including the detailed story of the coup that toppled his father from power!

US$27.95 print

A Whole New Navy: America's War in the Pacific

Miles Durr

The most comprehensive and detailed description of America's naval war in the Pacific ever—every battle, every ship, every task force and every task group from Pearl Harbor through the Japanese surrender! A must-have for the collection of every World War II buff!

US$29.95 print

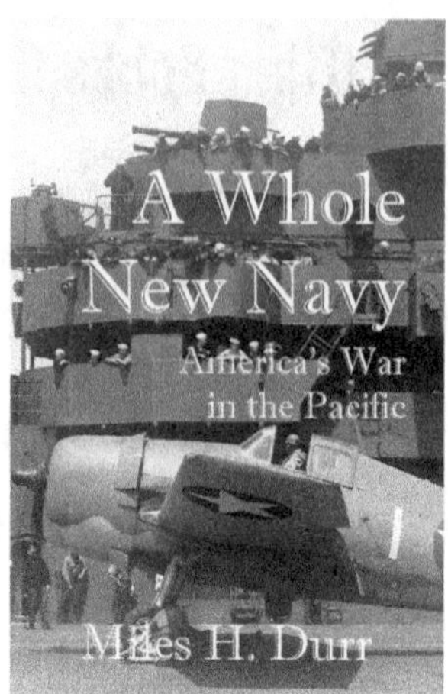

Improbable History: The Weird, the Obscure, and the Strangely Important

edited by Michael Dobson

From the birth of Western civilization to the rescue of Apollo 13, from the Leaning Tower of Pisa to Florence's Duomo, history has often turned on small, improbable details. Whatever happened to the ancient Samaritan people? Why did a fortuitous rainstorm allow the British to conquer India? How did an air raid in Italy lead to the development of chemotherapy? What happened when Albert Einstein met Adolf Hitler on the streets of Berlin? How did the Japanese manage to attack the US mainland using balloons? A cast of award-winning writers tackle some of the strangest tales in history!

US$19.95 print

The Letters of William Philip Schwartz 1842-1855

edited by John F. Schwartz

The 19th century soldier and adventurer William Philip Schwartz wrote a series of vivid and detailed letters chronicling his adventures in the Indian Wars, the Mexican-American War, the Gold Rush, and his term as Marine sergeant aboard the USS Constellation. A pioneer in photography, he took *the first known war photographs*. An unforgettable first-hand look into life in the 19th century!

US$17.95 print

Timespinner
Press

www.timespinnerpress.com

9 781976 215490